Talk's Cheap...
And So Am I

The Definitive, Authoritative, Official Guide to Cheapness

by

Ann M. Rogers

authorHOUSE™

1663 LIBERTY DRIVE, SUITE 200
BLOOMINGTON, INDIANA 47403
(800) 839-8640
WWW.AUTHORHOUSE.COM

First published by AuthorHouse 07/21/05

ISBN: 1-4208-6649-4 (e)
ISBN: 1-4208-6647-8 (sc)

Printed in the United States of America
Bloomington, Indiana

This book is printed on acid-free paper.

Dedication
& Acknowledgments

To my mother who taught me everything she knows.

To the M.D. whom had I married, this book would
not be necessary.

To the teacher who became my husband and made
this book and me everything we are.

Contents

Introduction

Talk's Cheap...And So Am I

I've always believed that the best things in life are free...and the rest should be purchased cheap.

It's a belief I've inherited and it's not as simple as it sounds. There are several ideas floating around in this general advocation of cheapness. There is the idea that not spending money is good in and of itself. There is also the idea that spending as little money as possible will eventually amount to saving big money.

There are many entrepreneurs (and politicians) who would dispute this philosophy that cheapness is a means towards achieving wealth.These people usually borrow enormous sums of money, which if things go according to plan, become even more enormous sums of money. This is in contradiction to the cheapness theory: that saving lots of itty bitty sums creates hordes of money. But, fortunately, in American, we are all free to pursue wealth in whatever manner we find plausible.

Like many people, I come by my cheapness biologically. My grandparents came to this country from Russia during that country's communist revolution. They were peasants who had the good sense to realize that only in a rich, capitalist country could cheapness have real meaning.

My father's parents had nothing when they arrived here. But through hard work and considerable cheapness, they were able to acquire a small apartment house and several other real estate holdings. They sold all their property before they died but, fortunately, my father inherited their attributes of thrift and hard work. And thankfully, he also got some of the loot.

Like cheap people everywhere, my father never expected the road ahead to be easy.

Why doesn't a cheap person just go out and buy, for example, a new car? Because a cheap person suspects that if he did go out and buy a new car, that's when his boss would suddenly turn to him and say, "Hey, bub, we all took a vote and decided that you're a waste of our money."

A cheap person is first and foremost a skeptic. A cheap person believes that just because things are good now doesn't mean that they will stay that way.

Being cheap is what you did in the times before welfare and social security, when a person had to rely on either his relatives or his neighbors to help out when times were rough. And just how helpful do you suppose neighbors and relatives would be towards people they regarded as spendthrifts? ("If you hadn't spent all your money on that fancy shamcy new car, you wouldn't need to come here and ask for our help!")

My father knew he had to work hard and be cheap to better himself. He worked his way through college and graduate school. And though his own parents were barely literate in English, my father earned a Ph.D. in biochemistry.

Today, as a first generation American, my father stands as a proud example of many things. Though he forgot his parent's ethnic heritage, rejected their religion, and can barely comprehend their language, let alone speak it, he is as thoroughly cheap as they were. And he tried his best to pass this family tradition on to his six children.

He also demonstrates that cheapness knows no logic. And that even a scientist, proficient in the scientific method and eminent enough to be listed in the Who's Who of American Men of Science, can, on the one hand, turn down the thermostat to 50 degrees in the dead of winter (because to him listening to the sound of a furnace kicking on is equivalent to hearing money burn) while, on the other hand, he can line his six children up in front of an ice cream truck and spend $20 on a few spoonfuls of ice cream.

My father also taught his children to be strong...even strong enough to be cheap. Since he was always annoyed by other people's overemphasis on superficial things, it wasn't out of character when one day, after doing a little painting around the house, he discovered he had paint enough left over to paint the car. So he did paint it, bumpers and all, with grey house paint. It was the family's only car and it wasn't a pretty sight. But every one of the six children---some in the middle of adolescence---had to endure being seen in that car.

My mother had a very different childhood than my father's. Her parents were middle-class storekeepers who were hard-working but extravagant. They were the first ones in their neighborhood to own a car. They also had a cleaning woman. My mother wasn't even exposed to cheapness until she married my father. But she must have had the genes for it. She took to it with unbounded zeal and today she is virtually indistinguishable from someone who was actually born cheap.

While both sides of my family were immigrants and both my parents were first generation Americans, my husband's family is close to being the original Americans settlers, farmers and cheapskates. In his family, the roots of cheapness run deep, strong and lean. There is no extravagance amongst these people. There are no mink coats, no Gucci handbags, no fancy baubles, no knick knacks. Here it is Sears and Wal-Mart all the way.

Conversation, naturally, takes place around the kitchen table and the talk here isn't about sports, fashions or daliances at the country club. It's about utility bills and the cost of parts to repair the tractor. The motto in this household is family, fidelity and frugality. And, since these folks know the price of an attorney, to them, that all means the same thing.

As a child, my husband learned how to be strong too. He and his three brothers had to take turn starting the family tractor. Since their parents couldn't afford a battery, the boys started the tractor by popping the clutch as it rolled downhill. Woe to him who failed to start it the first run. He had to push the tractor back up the hill to try again.

My husband says he never knew he was poor. It wasn't until he had grown up, that he looked back and realized how poor they were. And, it wasn't until he was in his thirties that he looked back and realized that not only were his parents poor, they were also cheap. When he was growing up, his parents were forced to work outside jobs while struggling to make a living as farmers. But, when they reached their forties and had paid off their farm, they suddenly had the leisure and money to express the inner selves they had so long ignored. And what they discovered was that they were living exactly the way they wanted to live. They discovered that while their earlier selves had been poor, their inner selves were cheap enough to like living that same way.

Having been both poor and cheap, my in-laws can tell you that there is a difference between the two. And, most people would agree.

Being poor is easy; anyone can do it. It doesn't take skill or effort. Many even regard it as resulting from the absence of skill and effort. Consequently, the last thing my in-laws wanted to look was poor. They always dressed up nice before they went into town. And, they bought as nice a car as they could afford.

Now to be considered cheap is another matter. To them, it is more a matter of good judgement. Sure they can afford to go to Red Lobster for their seafood meal. But if they enjoy the fish just as much at Long John Silvers, why not go there and pay less?

The crucial point between cheap and poor is that being cheap involves a choice. They have the money to play it either way. Therefore, they get to choose what gives them the best value for their dollar.

Call them poor and their feelings would be hurt to the very marrow; they have spent their entire lives working hard in order not to be poor. Call them cheap, however, and they'll probably agree. And then they'll explain that it was because they spent their whole lives working hard not to be poor that they are cheap.

Put my mother in the same defendant's box, and make the same accusations and you get a very different result. Accuse her of being cheap and she'll argue vehemently to the contrary. Though she has derived enormous pleasure from choosing where and how to spend her money, the power to choose has had its down side. She has had to contend with the "you never bought me a train set" syndrome from six children. Consequently, while she loves having the choice to spend, she simultaneously hates it too. Whereas, if only she had been poor, she would have been absolved of all responsibility.

It's true then that cheapness is understood as involving a choice. But what choice?

Some people consider a person generous if he chooses to spend his money on them; he's cheap if he doesn't, even though he may be extremely generous in spending money on himself.

Or, a person may be called cheap if he chooses to let other people buy him things he would never personally buy. Some people, for example, never order lobster except at a business lunch where someone else is footing the bill. A man I knew use to boast about how much he could chow down whenever his manager took him out to eat, thereby eliminating the need to eat any of his own food at home later.

However, there are two aspects to being cheap, both of which are equally important. The first part of being cheap is INTERNAL. It can be expressed as: Don't spend your own money. The second part, however, is EXTERNAL and it can be expressed as: Don't spend other people's money.

To be a true cheapskate requires integrity. It means you can't enjoy a ridiculously overpriced meal even if you're not paying for it. You can't enjoy it even if your worst enemy is paying for it. And being cheap means you probably consider all restaurant meals as ridiculously overpriced.

Being a true cheapskate means that you never just walk into a store and say, "I'll take it." And when someone is describing the great evening you're both going to have together, all you're thinking about is what it's going to cost you.

A genuine cheapskate worries about spending money. His daydreams consist of itemizing expenses and tabulating bills. His life's quest is to get his "money's worth", which means getting as much as possible while spending as little as possible.

A cheapskate never spends money without debating it. "To spend or not to spend" is always the question. And, for a true cheapskate, it's pretty much definite that as a general rule with very few exceptions, it is far better not to spend.

As previously stated, being cheap has meant different things in different time periods and in different countries. American Pseudo-Cheapness can be attributed to those people who do things like trade in their old, fully paid for Oldsmobile in order to buy a small import that gets twice the mileage. Only in order to buy that more economical import, they have to take out a car loan and their interest for just 6 months of that loan would pay for 10 years worth of extra gas on the Oldsmobile. American Pseudo-Cheapness also describes those people who max out their credit cards at 19% annual interest, but use 20 cent coupons when buying their groceries. It's also been called penny wise and pound foolish.

Traditional Cheapskates are the kind of people who keep their cars even after they're paid for and who shop for practical clothes at places like J. C. Penneys and Sears. The Traditional cheapskate women go to the beauty parlor only for weddings and funerals, and both these events are expected to occur only once per lifetime.

Pioneer cheapness applies to my in-laws. My mother-in-law does her own hair and they shop at Sears if there's a sale. She has a sewing machine to repair their clothes and she plants a vegetable garden every summer. They do their own maintenance work on their house and, in fact, my father-in-law built their house.

Lastly, there is the category of Gulag Cheap. People who are Gulag Cheapskates either live in Siberia or act as though they do. Gulag cheapskates don't go to the beauty parlor. They may or may not have hair; they don't know or care. They want nothing; they buy nothing. Now they're CHEAP.

If you are a true, honest-to-goodness, Traditional, Pioneer or Gulag cheapskate, you can't disguise yourself. And why should you? You should be proud to be cheap.

Being cheap makes sense for many reasons. It makes good financial sense. We can't all get loans for millions or billions of dollars from the bank or government. We have to learn to live within a budget. We have to learn to work hard and practice rigorous economy. We have to learn to climb out from under the oppression of material possessions, out from under the weight of monthly payments. With will power, an eye on higher goals and a clamp on our checkbook, we can slowly but surely attain that euphoric and tranquil state known as solvency.

I explain the rationale of being cheap to my children, how cheapness makes good economic sense, and that the money not spent today will become something bigger and better tomorrow. I tell them that someday, because of my financial strategy, we'll all be rich.

At that point, they usually eye me suspiciously. "But mom," they say, "you'll still be cheap."

I certainly hope so.

Part One

General Guidelines and Buylines

Chapter One

You Too Should Be Cheap

Some lucky people are naturally thin; truly lucky people are naturally cheap.

But if you're not a natural cheapskate, don't give up hope. It is possible to learn to be cheap.

However, you may be asking yourself why you should bother. You may spout some bromide about eating and drinking today because tomorrow you may die, which all sounds fine and dandy unless you suffer the ill-fortune of not dying. What then?

Barbara, a blonde, forty-two year old, knows what happens. She is a nurse who worked in a nursing home for many years. It was there she learned that the government didn't take over the payments of the old people in the home until their own assets were wiped out. From that, Barbara might have concluded: 1. don't ever go to a nursing home 2. if you do go to a nursing home, sell everything you've got and start giving it to your children or 3. don't save any money. Barbara opted for number 3.

She went on a spending spree; she married and divorced 2 times. During her fourth marriage, she was finally settled into a beautiful home and, to all appearances, she finally had everything. But the overspending and thriftlessness continued and she lost it all. Her husband was accused of embezzlement, probably to satisfy Barbara's insatiable thirst for blowing those wads, and today, all their income is spoken for--from paying past debts to past embezzlements.

The rationale for being cheap is that the future is unknown. Of course, the rationale for being a spendthrift is also that the future is unknown. However, there are other rationales for being cheap. First and foremost, it strengthens your character. You must learn to find pleasure and enjoyment within yourself because you can't spend the money to find it any place else. You can't hire someone to tell you how and when to exercise; you have to exercise all by yourself. You can't hire a psychologist to listen to your problems; you have to talk to and listen to yourself.

It's environmentally sound to be cheap. Cheap people don't go to Venice to breathe on and destroy all the wonderful architecture and art works. Cheap people are not in Egypt throwing their trash and stomping about the Pyramids. Cheap people do not constitute the ugly Americans that the French supposedly hate. Because cheap people don't go any place. They're home, sitting on the couch, and about the most ecological damage they do is to periodically flush the toilet. And even then, they make sure everyone in the house has used it first.

Are cheap people faddish? They wait until the fad is over before they'll even consider buying whatever it is.

Are cheap people plugging up the roads or the bathrooms when there's a rock concert, football game or some other big event in town? Cheap people don't buy tickets to anything...not even the lottery.

Cheapskates also make great neighbors. They never keep up with the Jones or anyone else. They don't have the fanciest car in the neighborhood. They don't own a motorhome, a boat or a plane. They don't put pressure on anyone to keep up with them.

There's an awful lot of good things to be said for cheap people as well as in favor of being cheap. Cheap people are not drug addicts. Cheap people don't sit at a bar scarfing down drinks. A cheap people knows better than to spend money to stick things up his nose or down his throat; he sticks his money where it belongs...in the bank accruing interest.

Yes, cheap people are good people. They are the salt of the earth....because salt is cheap too.

Chapter Two

Some Cheap Rules of Thumb

The first rule is:

It's not what you earn that counts, it's what you spend.

Jake, for example, doesn't earn much above minimum wage as a food service worker. He rents a studio apartment for about $300 monthly and still manages to save several hundred dollars every month. How does he do it? He doesn't own a car but lives close enough to walk to work. He doesn't turn his hot water heater on until a half hour before he takes a bath. He doesn't have a phone. He is cheap---borderline Gulag. He's also solvent. And he probably has more money in his bank account than do most people who earn ten times what he does. That's because he understands that first rule of being cheap. What you earn isn't as important as what you don't spend.

The second important rule is:

Don't spend it.

Don't spend it unless you really, really, honest-to-goodness need it.

This brings up the important philosophical discussion on what a person really needs. The word "need" is used rather glibly in these times. Many years ago, when a person said that he needed a new pair of pants, you could feel confident that it was necessary because the person had either outgrown the old ones or outlasted them. But nowadays, need is mistakely used for want. And though advertisers and the media are blamed for creating this confusion between need and want, let's put the blame where it belongs...squarely on the person doing the buying.

To set the record straight on some important issues:

First, brides do not need weddings. It is perfectly possible to get married (and even stay married) without spending more than, say, $20. (I'm proud to say my own particular marriage ceremony cost far less than that.) And, not spending your life savings on your little girl doesn't mean you don't love her. As will be elaborated on in later chapters, one of the good things about being cheap is that love is treated as a purely spiritual thing not to be confused with or translated into material possessions.

Other things that aren't needed are new cars, memberships to a health spa, boats, pools, and a 4-5 bedroom colonial with a 2 car garage.

Confusing need with want can cause great damage, sometimes irreversible damage particularly to your bank account.

One young couple was just starting out their marriage with only a few hundred dollars in the bank. The husband was about eighteen years old and not earning much in the military. The wife was about the same age and looking for a job. They were barely making ends meet while renting an overpriced apartment in the Cheap People's Hell known as southern California. Yet, the wife spent over a hundred dollars of their little nest egg because she believed all married couples needed this something. A bed? No. A stereo system? No again. A set of china. You got it. That's right. She believed every married couple needs a set of china. And she didn't even clear this purchase with her husband first. (Wish that china was unbreakable.)

Needs are, in fact, rather simple. Food, water, shelter. Clothes are a good idea too---although without them, you'll be able to get the other three necessities free of charge.

Wants can get complicated. They can range from wanting pants, shirt and shoes in matching leather to wanting a smoothly paved tennis court with night lighting.

The whole issue is further complicated by people who gladly sacrifice what they clearly need in order to get something they want. You hear about people who do without heat in order to afford tickets to the opera. Or people scrimp on their lunches in order to buy a special dress. So, in a sense, this makes some wants a greater need than some needs.

What you need may not be what you want. Or you may want what you don't need or you may want what you need and so much else that you can't possibly keep what you need or want.

But the general rule as to needs and wants is really rather simple.

Whatever it is, need or want, if you positively have to get it, at least spend as little as possible doing it.

Chapter Three

Do I Have to Bake Bread?

There is concern amongst cheapskates and would-be cheapskates on just how much work being cheap entails. They worry whether they are working hard enough at being cheap. They are plagued by doubts as to just how much physical labor being cheap demands.

In short, they want to know the answer to that fundamental question:

Should they bake their own bread?

It might help them to know that there are two separate and distinct groups of cheapskates. There are the rural cheapskates who believe that the only way to get something cheap is to do it or grow it yourself. But then, there is also the group of urban cheapskates who believe that the only way to get something cheap is to shop around for it.

Many rural cheapskates were once urban cheapskates. However, when they finally took the big step and bought that undervalued farm house, they were suddenly overcome by the yearning to grow vegetables, bake bread and can beans. They also start to sew their own clothes, knit their own scarfs, and build their own furniture. The main thing that distinguishes them from the original pioneers who were also rural cheapskates is that today's rural cheapskates get so much pleasure out of doing all this.

Urban cheapskates, on the other hand, believe they can do just as well (if not better) than the rural cheapskate does in saving money. While the rural cheapskate's skill is in his hands, the urban cheapskate's is in his feet. If your prices aren't good, he can go elsewhere, thank you.

Urban or rural. The original pioneer cheapskates didn't have achoice. You do.

Chapter Four

Ask The Cheapskate

Q: Should I give money to charity?

A: Yes, definitely. (And for the record, I'm open to donations.)

Q: Is cheapness learned or is it genetic?

A: The answer to this is not yet known and unfortunately, no one has volunteered to finance a study.

Q: Are there any cheapskates in politics?

A: You're kidding, right?

Q: Should I continue to shop at a store with excellent prices even though the salespeople are rude?

A: No one said it was easy to be cheap. Be strong, continue to shop there and may the bargains be with you.

Q: Must a cheap woman work outside the home?

A: Yes. This is necessary since no one has yet found a way to mow the lawn, change the car's oil, or paint the exterior of the house while sitting inside on the couch.

Q: Is there a cheap pet? If so, what is it?
A: Yes. Your neighbor's.

Q: How many cheapskates does it take to change a lightbulb?
A: Only one. But the more important question is how much did the lightbulb cost and is that the best you can do.

Chapter Five

Dare To Be Cheap

It is impossible to even consider being cheap without dealing with the psychological aspect of it.

Sure, you may have a low enough income to warrant being cheap, but do you have what it takes mentally?

Are you tough enough?

Being cheap in today's day and age sometimes feels like you're driving a rusty, dented old Dodge down the highway of life when everyone else is driving a new BMW.

Jane knows. She's been driving her old Dod wagon (it's a Dodge but the "g" and "e" have fallen off over the years) in her nice suburban neighbor for years. Every other mother has either a new minivan, a nice Mercedes or a shiny 4 wheel drive. When Jane picks up her kids at the nearby elementary school amongst all those fashionable vehicles, her rusty wagon tends to stand out like a pimple on a cover girl's face. It's a blemish on the neighborhood.

Sure Jane knows that she and her husband George could afford a new car. They could go down today and trade their old Dod in for something with a complete set of letters. They could trade in a zero monthly payment for a payment of several hundred dollars. They could trade in looking poor with appearing rich. And let's face it, it would be easy to do.

A lot of people take this route. They work themselves into tremendous debt as they frantically try to show everyone how rich they are.

Barry and Lisa, who are married, employed in low paying jobs and have 3 children, decided to trade in their old junker for a nicer, used car. They were just tired of looking poor. As a consequence, when the owner of the house they were renting offered to sell it to them before putting it on the market, they couldn't afford to accept his generous terms. They were too poor from trying to look rich. Yet, had they the mental toughness to look a little poorer, they might have become a little richer. Instead, when the house was sold, they had to move into a smaller townhouse that rented for much more and wasn't nearly as nice.

Yet, Harry and Betty, a retired couple in their fifties, can appreciate why Barry and Lisa did what they did. Harry and Betty remember watching their neighbors go away on vacation each year while they stayed home. Those neighbors were always doing things that Harry and Betty didn't do because they were saving their money. It was difficult at the time, Harry recalls. They wondered whether they were doing the right thing or not. But now, years later, Harry notes that those neighbors are still having to work to make ends meet.

The problem is that the future is unknown. You cannot know now whether your financial game plan of thrift and deprivation is going to pay off. That's precisely why it takes mental toughness. Since you're also going against the general behavior of most people, you may feel like you're swimming upstream while everyone else is floating peacefully down...on inner tubes. You're out there fighting the current and wondering why. But appearances are deceiving. They may look happy in their new cars, expensive homes fully furnished with actual store-bought furniture; they may even be happy. But they shouldn't be happy. They're too much in debt to be happy. It's only because they're hopelessly stupid that they're happy.

On the other hand, the curse of being smart is that you can't be happy based on appearances alone. You can't be satisfied with showing a good front to the world while knowing your back side is bare. You want something more; you want substance; you want solvency.

"Buy now, pay later" is the motto of folks with no will power. They use their mortality as an excuse to fulfill their every whim. They lack the discipline and strenght to forgo therich look in order to achieve a rich bank account.

But to drive that old junker out among the spanking new automobiles, to wear the same clothes day in and day out, to eat out on your own back patio, and to spend your vacation lolling on the couch, now that takes real courage.

Chapter Six

You Get What You Pay For: Cliche, Myth

Or Wishful Thinking

"You get what you pay for" expresses the idea that something more expensive is a better product than something less expensive. It's the idea that if the product is made out of tyraneum, that the more expensive product will be richer in tyraneum.

You'd think that if there's anything that the automobile industry in this country succeeded in doing, it was in dispelling the myth that more expensive means better.

It is possible that if you're talking about brownies, for example, that the more expensive brownie may have more sugar, milk and butter in it than the less expensive brownie. But that doesn't mean that you'll like it better. Doug, a father of four grew up on Hostess's Twinkies and cupcakes and he absolutely hates expensive bakery items. Give him a creme filled eclair from one of the bakeries in your less prestigious grocery stores and he is in heaven.

Give him the same item made of the finest ingredients and costing twice as much from a fancy french bakery and it just isn't the same thing. His tastes are pedestrian; he admits it. But the fact is that he prefers what he gets when he doesn't pay as much for it.

And then there is another example to consider. Suppose you have two women equally in love with their husbands, equally good mothers except that one woman is always out shopping and spending money while the other isn't. Is the one who costs more here BETTER than the one who costs less? Wouldn't the expression "You get what you pay for" be meant ironically in this situation as in "You wanted such a hot shot wife, now pay for it."

There are therefore a few possibilities here. What you get when you pay for it may be exactly what you want; what you get when you pay for it may not be what you want; and what you get when you pay for it may be a disaster.

However, a confident shopper believes that getting a good product at a low price is not an impossibility as the slogan "You get what you pay for" implies. It's just a matter of skill, patience and intelligence. In short, it's the difference between a good shopper and a bad one.

Part Two

From Cheap Kisses to Cheap Kids

Chapter Seven

The Cheap Dating Game

The one thing no one ever teaches you about love is that it shouldn't be expensive.

Both men and women seem to have difficulty believing this.

Many women seem to take a special delight in having men spend money on them. They believe that there's a correlation between how much money is spent on them and how much they're worth. Following this logic, nothing would make them happier than to see an extremely wealthy man plunge into bankruptcy proceedings on their account.

A woman who equates love with spending money is bound to be a very expensive pain in the wallet. Tell her you love her and she'll be looking for a fur coat or diamond ring to prove it. To her, the language of love translates into goods of commerce.

There are also men like this. There are men who are waiting to throw their money out on some woman. They seem to consider spending the natural consequence of romance. The further they plunge into love, the deeper they expect to plunge into their checking account.

A Navy enlisted man named Bruce spent close to a weeks pay for one night courting a woman he was very likely never to see again. The woman, Alise, was in town visiting her brother and Bruce went head over heels for her. Or more accurately, heels over head for her...because that's the position necessary to empty his pockets. And he probably did more than empty his pockets after the evening out was over. He bought her an expensive gold bracelet before the cab arrived to take them to the restaurant. And why did he hire a cab? He was too poor to own a car.

It might be argued that Bruce and Alise deserved each other. She boasted of all the money he was spending on her, and the idiot kept wanting to spend it. If these two ever declared their love for each other, they'd probably be declaring bankruptcy soon after.

It's true that some people think theatrics are necessary to prove true love. You have to wonder if people like this have seen too many movies. They think talking love requires using their credit card. They confuse romantic "give and take" with actually giving and taking things.

A twice divorced man named Rick decided he was going to ask Claire to marry him. Rick is a hard-working man with two children who has never been extravagant in his life, except when it comes to women.

So he didn't just go over to Claire's house and ask her to marry him. And he didn't go out to eat with her and ask her to marry him. He rented an airplane, bought her a dozen roses and while they're up in the airplane sipping champagne, he asked her to marry him.

And she said no.

As Rick was telling me this story, I think he was feeling rather happy with himself. I think he was thinking that he is a very romantic fellow.

A sentiment I quickly destroyed.

What a waste of money, I said.

Love doesn't require spending money. It simply does not.

The greatest love stories of all times have nothing whatsoever to do with spending any money. Did Romeo spend money on Juliet? Did he take her out to eat at a French restaurant? Buy her candy or flowers? Did his courting her in any way diminish the size of his bank account? Of course not. In fact, had any kind of cash expenditures taken place, the whole image of pure, untarnished love would have been destroyed.

For true love to exist it has to be independent of the wealth of the parties. That's the whole point of the wedding vows "for richer or poorer". Love is spiritual, as opposed to material, which means that love can exist---in fact, will exist---without candy, fur, jewelry, flowers, maid service or vacations.

But the biggest problem with love is not in defining it, it's in finding it. It's in sifting through all those would-be diamonds for that glorious, contented lump of coal.

Chapter Eight

Cheap Sex

Although love can be gotten cheap, sex can't.

Sex costs money because birth control costs money. Of course, abstinence doesn't involve any money but then it doesn't involve any sex either. On the other hand, the rhythm method of birth control involves some sex and no money, and this method may be the one of choice for those who prefer to have their hearts yearning and their sex cheap.

Maureen has a regular menstrual cycle of 28 days although it can get as long as 31 days and as short as 26 days. Maureen determines her period of abstinence by subtracting 18 days from 31 and 11 days from 26. So, she tells her husband Teddy that she has a headache from day 8 to day 20 of each cycle. That gives Teddy 13 days without sex...with Maureen, that is, and approximately 15 days with sex. Effectiveness of this method is 86%, though the divorce rate is even higher. Cheapness rate is 100% (unless you get pregnant, in which case cheapness drops to 0%).

The birth control pill is considered the most effective method, but it is not the cheapest. When you're on the pill, you've always got birth control. So you're actually paying for birth control whether or not you're using it. This is offensive to any cheap person's sensibilities. To get your money's worth out of this method requires an enormous amount of sexual activity.

Another drawback to the pill is that it requires regular visits to the doctor's office to get the prescription. You have to pay someone in order to pay someone for the birth control pills. Involving the middleman-medical man in a business transaction drives up the cost, not to mention the expenditure of time and effort.

There are also mechanical contraceptives such as the condom and diaphragm. The diaphragm must be fitted and there goes more money to a third party. And if your weight doesn't remain fairly constant, you'll need one for when you're fat, medium and thin. There is the contraceptive sponge, which works like a diaphragm except one size fits all. One sponge is good for 24 hours no matter how much sex takes place during that time. It isn't as cheap as abstinence but it is cheaper than pregnancy. And there are ways to get your money's worth.

What Joanna does is put her sponge in late Friday night. That makes it good from 11:30 pm Friday until 11:30 pm Saturday. Instead of using one sponge for sex on Friday and another sponge for sex on Saturday, Joanna gets 2 nights for the price of one sponge.

Getting sterilized is another increasingly popular method. It's not free, though it does prevent the incurrence of new expenses.

Fortunately, Mother Nature knew what it was doing.

Women do get less fertile as the years pass and around the corner, not too far out of sight, is free birth control for each and every one of them.

Hurrah for menopause!

Chapter Nine

A Good Wife is a Cheap Wife

Charlie, who sells cars for a living, likes to refer to his wife affectionately as his Porsche.

A cheap man doesn't want to do this. It would be much wiser for a cheap man to refer to his wife as perhaps his Ford. Preferably, his reliable old Ford.

Just think of the upkeep of a Porsche. Someone who is called a Porsche is going to go to the beauty parlor at least once a week. She's going to belong to a health club. She's going to go shopping to keep her slim lines looking elegant.

But call a woman an old Ford and she'll probably cut her own hair, walk around in 5 year old clothes and get her exercise running to catch the bus for work.

It was once believed that a wife was a husband's showpiece. He used her to show how successful he was. Consequently, he decked her out in jewels and furs. He put her in the most luxurious car he could almost afford and all she was supposed to do was drive that luxury car around and spend his money. She didn't have to do anything else precisely because he was so successful.

Fortunately, with cheap men, this idea was always passe.

With cheap men, women have always been equals.

Andrea knows all about being an equal. Her husband Jim drives the nicer looking car to work while she gets the clunker. Since he makes more money at his job than she does at hers, it's more important that he have the reliable car as his transportation. And she'll never forget the time her car broke down in the middle of an intersection in the pouring rain. She had left for work before her husband and she remembers sitting in her car thankful that Jim would be along any minute. When she finally spotted him, she watched with relief as he pulled his car over and ran to her. "For God's sakes," he greeted her as the rain drenched him, "Don't you know you're supposed to push your car to the side of the road?"

It reminded Andrea immediately of what she loved most about Jim. He was always a real woman's libber. No double standard for him. Just one cheap standard for everyone.

Jim and Andrea have never quarrelled about money. They have always shared the same philosophy in regards to money: to not spend it. Jim knows better than to ever purchase Andrea a present of any kind. She wouldn't appreciate the gesture. The last thing she'd want is a material symbol of his love, particularly one that had to be paid for out of their bank account.

Andrea considers herself a good wife, the best wife. She mows the lawn and doesn't hire help to clean the house. She does the cooking and takes care of the children. She feeds the pets and does no other shopping but the food shopping.

It's true that she doesn't wear make-up and her body hasn't been toned in an aerobics class. She owns no jewelry and her hair looks a mess. Her clothes don't have fancy labels, her car is crummy and her house isn't a show place. But her bank account...now that's something.

Chapter Ten

Raising Cheap Kids Cheap

Thriftiness is, unfortunately, a sophisticated concept not even many grown-ups seem to understand. It involves the idea of delayed gratification. The idea is that in putting off today's pleasure for the possibility of tommorrow's pleasure must become a pleasure in itself.

The idea of thriftiness and delayed gratification does not become an issue while the children are still very young. Here the parents make all the decisions and the children are blissfully ignorant of the outside world. If they see a cookie, they may want a cookie. Even if they don't see a cookie, as long as they've seen a cookie, they may want a cookie. But they haven't yet acquired the subtle perception and mental skills required to want a neon colored, 15 speed mountain bike.

Matching furniture, new wallpaper, stuffed animals, fancy clothes....it is satisfying the parents' wants that can make having a baby expensive.

Younger children seem to naturally imitate their parents. Janette Wilson remembers affectionately how her little ones learned first to say, "mommy" and "daddy" and "too much".

Older children are a different story. Once they start to go to school, they start to learn. And what they learn first and best is what anyone else has that they don't have.

You will have to do what you can to keep the child up to par with his peers. This is a good reason for not living in a wealthy neighborhood. While you may have the strength to be cheap, your children will not. They don't know about bank accounts; they don't know about interest payments. All they know is that their friends have cool stuff and they don't.

The rule for getting only what you need is suspended when it comes to children. While the fact is that, physically, children need very little. They have an infinite number of wants and some of those wants are actually needs because without them, the child will not grow up healthy and happy. Of course, it is impossible for any parent to know which want is the crucial one. You don't find out until the child is grown up and then they turn to you one day and say, "you never bought me a train set." Of course, had you know then that the train set was the crucial want/need, you would have willingly bought it. But it is impossible to know you should have bought it until years later when it is no longer necessary to buy it.

Now you can buy the child each and everything they want so that you will hopefully eliminate that possibility. But very few parents can afford to do this. And the likelihood is that even if you did this, the child would then complain that you bought him too much.

Satisfying the child's wants---at least to some extent---is necessary. However, it isn't necessary to buy children only new toys. If you can find what the child wants at garage sales, then that's great. Unfortunately, your child is likely to want a toy when everyone else wants it. This means that you're going to end up buying toys new, which is not a pleasant experience.

Sue knows. She has spent more money on Barbie's clothes than she has on her clothes. Barbie has designer outfits; Susie doesn't. Barbie has matching hats and shoes; Susie can't afford it. Barbie has a motor home and a spa and a pool; Susie has none of these. Although Susie sometimes thinks that she would have a little more if only Barbie had a little less.

But the fact is that there is much to enjoy in having children. They are fun, inquisitive and perceptive. And they get to go places you don't go and hear things you don't get to hear.

Andrea derives all sorts of fun from her children. She finds out what happened at school that day; she finds out what is going on at the neighbor's house. She found out the neighbors were getting a divorce because their child told her children.

Andrea teaches her children to behave properly whenever they go into a neighbor's house. That means they don't fight; they don't touch anything that's breakable; and they come home prepared to draw the entire floor plan.

Andrea herself was raised the same way. She knew French provincial furniture before she knew her A, B, C's. She knew a colonial from a ranch, what a mansard roof was and the layout of a central floor plan. And she knew nothing got her mother's attention as much as telling her what her friends' parents did for a living.

In the end, however, there are no guarantees. Many a tightfisted family has produced extravagant children. And yet, it is hopeful to note that out of many an extravagant family has come a precious little cheapskate.

Some Rules Which May or May Not Work

Talk about money.

When the child says he wants something, ask how much it costs. The child will learn to understand that there is an association between the object's price and his chances of ever getting the object.

Talk about money as a reward for work and reward the child for his work.

Sue pays her children to take piano lessons. Sue pays her child to lend each other clothes. Though many people object to this kind of family wheeling and dealing, Sue believes she is teaching her children that money is a means of negotiating. It's not a substitute for love or attention. It's just a means to an end....specifically, the end of arguments.

Talk about relative prices and saving money for something in the future.

Children often spend their money in what appears to be foolishly. They will go to the convenience store and get one lollipop at the price of what half a bag costs in a discount department store. You might want to mention this to them. But you don't want to reprimand them. You don't want them to associate heartache, guilt and unhappiness with spending money....or do you?

Chapter Eleven

The A, B, C's To Shop By

Affordable
Bargain, Bonus, Budget
Clearance, Coupons
Discounted
End of Season
Free
Going out of business
Half-price
Irregular
Junk
K-Mart
Low Prices
Marked Down
No reasonable offer refused
Overstocked
Priced to go
Quality merchandise
Rock Bottom
Sale, savings, specials
Thrift store
Unbelievable low prices

Value
Wholesale
X-tra low prices
Yard Sale
Zero Interest

But no matter what words they use, your most important words are always the same. "How much?"

Chapter Twelve

Money Talks; Some People Don't

Most people would find it less awkward to have their friends see them naked than to have their friends see them balancing their checkbook. They'd rather talk about how much weight they've gained in the past year than how much money they have in the bank.

Bill and Sarah were good friends throughout college. They talked about everything together, which was why Sarah couldn't understand it when Bill got his first job and wouldn't tell her what he was earning. It was a good job; it was in his field of expertise. So what was the problem?

That was when Sarah first realized that Bill wasn't like her. And when he wouldn't even tell her how much he had paid for the car he was going to drive to work in, she knew with certainty that he was different. He belonged to another group of people, the group of people who DON'T TALK MONEY.

Sarah had never met anyone who belonged to that group before. Having grown up in New York, she thought that everyone talked money. When she was out walking and waiting to cross the street, all the people around her talked money. "My landlord is raising my rent $15 a month, can you believe it?" And she knew her parents talked money. "A gallon of milk went up 25 cents", "the russet potatoes were on sale for 5 pounds for $1" and similar topics could keep everyone conversing during an entire meal. And when she went out shopping with her mother, the people there all talked money. "That one is $14.99 but you can buy 2 for $25." Her relatives also talked money. "My water bill was $40 for last month and I only take one bath a day and I fill the tub up 4 inches from the bottom."

After her experience with Bill, Sarah wanted to determine right away which group the people she met belonged to. She'd steer the conversation ever so subtly to financial topics as, for example, "how much did you pay for your house?" and then, immediately, she'd know which group the person belonged in.

Talking money was once considered crass and low-brow. Aristocrats didn't talk about money because they didn't have to. They inherited their position and their wealth, which made them topics of no real interest. But when people who work for a living refuse to talk about money--even with their close relatives and friends, it can't be because money isn't important. If money isn't important, why are they out working to get it?

It's almost as though money is too important to talk about. It's as though they believe that you are what you earn.

While capitalism is a great system, it proves everyday that there is no perfect system for dispensing wealth. If the system was perfect, then farmers who make food would earn more than legislators who make nothing. And everyone can point to a number of movie stars and other celebrities who can't act, sing or do any of the things that they're being paid so much to do. Think of one of them (Cher, for example, or Ali Macgraw) and you'll realize that while money is important, you can't use it as a gauge to determine your worth. Well, actually, you can but you'll find the experience very depressing.

People who talk money have its value in perspective. Money is used to determine the value of objects, not people. You just can't put a price on the value of a whole person....especially a person who's a cheapskate.

Chapter Thirteen

Welcome to the Neighborhood Questionaire

1. You bought your house for: a. $50,000 -$100,000 b. $100,000-$150,000 c. $150,000-$200,000 d. $200,000-$250,000 e. fill in the exact amount_____.

2. What do you do for a living?

3. What does your spouse do for a living?

4. Your total income is: a. 0 -$20,000 b. $20,000 -$30,000 c. $30,000-$40,000 d. $40,000-$50,000 e.$50,000-$60,000 f.$60,000-$70,000 g.$70,000-more than you'll ever see.

5. Your mortgage payments are:

6. Your car payments are:

7. You would characterize your debt as being: a. very little b. manageable c. up to your eyeballs d. pre-chapter 7 bankruptcy

8. Do you have any savings? How much?

An IRA? Stocks?

9. Anything else you'd like to add to help illuminate your general economic status would be greatly appreciated.

Chapter Fourteen

Telephone Lines are Thicker Than Blood or Water

Once upon a time, blood was thicker than water. But then, the telephone system was developed.

Now, in many families, relationships develop that have nothing to do with blood lines and everything to do with telephone lines. It isn't a question of who is your closest relative. It's a question of who is your local phone call.

April is the mother of 4 daughters, all living within a 30 mile radius of her. April loves all her daughters dearly. But she seldom talks to Deidre, even though Deidre is the mother of her two grandchildren. She seldom talks to Floreen, though Floreen is her youngest. And she seldom talks to Ingrid, even though Ingrid has an exciting career in advertising. She only talks regularly to Lucille and it's not because Lucille is doing anything special that none of the other three girls are doing. It's because only Lucille is a local phone call.

While Lucille is a local call to her mother April and Lucille's friend Beth is a local call to April, Beth is not a local call to Lucille. Consequently, when Lucille has a message to give to Beth, she calls April. Then April calls Beth and then April calls Lucille.

Now while Floreen is just a few miles north of April, she is out of local calling range. Still it isn't quite long distance either. It's only 13 miles from Floreen's house to April's house and it's under the local phone company. And it is a very expensive thirteen miles. It is cheaper per mile for Floreen to call someone on the exact opposite coast than to call April.

Gee, no GTE.

Because of the way the phone system operates, Floreen has established a rather close relationship with Mabel. Mabel isn't a relative, but she is a local phone call. And, Mabel's sister Ruth is a friend of Beth. And consequently, what April tells Beth who tells Ruth who tells Mabel eventually finds its way to Floreen.

Ingrid is also not a local phone call to Floreen, except when she's at work and Floreen is at work. Their work numbers are local phone calls. But if Floreen can't get hold of Ingrid, who has a very busy schedule, then she leaves a message with her secretary Charlene. As a consequence, Charlene and Floreen have become quite good friends.

Deidre's mother-in-law is Karen Sue and, thankfully, Karen Sue is not a local phone call to Deidre. However Karen Sue's first cousin is Pamela and Pamela's best friend is Margaret and Margaret is a local phone call to Deidre. And not only that, but Pamela is friends with Amy who is Beth's very own mother. So, April tells Beth who tells Amy who tells Pamela who tells Margaret who tells Deidre.

And that's why sometimes when Katie and Rachel, Deidre's children and April's grandchildren, say their prayers at night, they ask whether talking to God is a local call.

Part Three

Cheap Mirth and Girth

Chapter Fifteen

Eating Out Without Paying Out

THE TEN COMMANDMENTS

Commandment One.

THOU SHALT NOT USE VENDING MACHINES.

Vending machines have an enormous attraction to children but not Mary's children. She taught her four children the first commandment of eating out before they were even able to say, "I want that." Mary herself could be lying in the desert dying of thirst and she wouldn't put a coin into a vending machine selling drinks next to her. Her last words before she died would be, "I could buy a whole quart for the price of that tiny thing."

It is never economical to buy from a vending machine. Vending machines sell convenience and if there's anything a cheapskate is willing to put up with to save money, it's a little inconvenience. So what if you're dying of hunger, it's a mere 10 miles to a supermarket and then you can buy a whole bag of pretzels for the price of that handful.

Commandment Two

THOU SHALT NOT BUY FROM ANYTHING ON WHEELS.

Same theory here as with the vending machines. They are selling convenience for people who have so much money in theirpockets that they can afford to throw it out. It's true that the hot dog at the cart is cheaper than going into a coffee shop and eating something. But bringing your lunch is even a better bargain.

Commandment Three

THOU SHALT NOT EAT IN PICTURESQUE LOCATIONS.

You can bet if you're eating overlooking the ocean or you're eating in an old mill that use to crank out flour a hundred years ago, then you're paying extra for it.

Commandment Four

THOU SHALT NOT EAT IN TOURIST ATTRACTIONS (OR MALLS.)

Related to the previous one. Have you ever checked the price of an ordinary hamburger in close proximity to a tourist attraction? Can it be that they are selling them special cows?

Commandment Five

THOU SHALT NOT EAT AT THE TOP OF BUILDINGS.

For some reason, the higher up in the air you get, the higher your bill gets. They might be hoping that the lack of oxygen will impair your sensibilities.

Commandment Six

THOU SHALT NOT EAT ANYPLACE WHERE YOU DON'T PARK YOUR OWN
CAR

Commandment Seven

THOU SHALT NOT EAT AT FRENCH RESTAURANTS.

John and Lee, teenagers, were out on a date and decided to eat at a French restaurant. Such tiny portions and so much money. While John's dad was generous about John's spending, he wouldn't have understood paying a credit card bill of $75 for two non-wage-earning adults to eat out. So John told his dad that it was actually a bill for 2 other couples, who reimbursed him for their share. John went on to become a lawyer so he can afford to continue eating at French restaurants. Lee went on to become a cheapskate and she refers to that experience in the French restaurant whenever she argues against the idea that you get what you pay for.

Commandment Eight

THOU SHALT NOT EAT AT ANY RESTAURANT IN NEW YORK OR OTHER
BIG CITIES.

The idea is simple. Big city=big bill.

Commandment Nine

THOU SHALT NOT ORDER DRINKS.
If you need alcohol in order to relax when you're eating out, then it would be a lot less expensive to just stay home and restup on the couch.

Commandment Ten

THOU SHALT EAT AT BUFFETS.
Jean and Herb love to eat at the all-you-can-eat places. Whenever they go some place new, they look up restaurants in the phone book and they visit the ones with the stuff your face buffets. They've been at buffets all over the country. For them, it's forget the tourist attractions; where's the nearest smorgasbord?

Chapter Sixteen

Getting Away and
Not Giving it Away

DISNEY WORLD

The cheapskate's guide to Disney World contains three important rules.

Rule 1: Don't Go.

Rule 2: If you have to go, don't eat.

Rule 3: If you have to eat, don't eat the ice cream bars.

Jan laughed the first time she saw the prices on the ice cream carts. She knew that no one would be insane enough to pay those prices and she was glad. If only Walt Disney had been alive, she thought, he wouldn't have allowed this to go on. But as the morning hours passed, Jan became more and more depressed. Her fellow human beings were weak, weak beings, she decided as she watched more and more pass with ice cream bars held high in their hands. She felt herself fill with disgust. And then she turned around and found her own husband purchasing four bars.

There is, of course, a reason that amusement parks exist. Amusement parks exist solely because of capitalism. In a capitalist economy, there is a division of labor. No longer must people work day and night just to survive. Not everyone has to worry anymore about the crops failing. They don't have to worry about finding wood for their stove. Consequently, they want to go to an amusement part, the cost of which wipes out their entire bank account so that they can again experience that primal fear.

It is simply not true that everyone in the universe wants to go to Disney World. Ilene would never go. Ilene doesn't believe that anything truly fun can cost that much money. Ilene can get more pleasure and excitement in one blue light special at K-Mart than a whole day spent at Disney World. The only way she'd ever go was if someone gave her the tickets free and made it a condition that she couldn't turn around and sell them.

The fact is that Disney World is truly the realization of a child's viewpoint. The fun lasts for about five minutes. At the end of the day, he and everyone else is sick enough to throw up. And to do it all requires spending about a zillion times more than it's actually worth.

It isn't true that you haven't lived unless you've been to Disney World. You'll not only have lived, you'll have some money to prove it.

Las Vegas

The great thing about Vegas is that other people gamble there. That makes lots of thing cheap. Steak meals for nothing much. And buffets. Jean and Herb love the buffets. And heck, they even hand out money at some places. That's because they think you're stupid. They think that they'll give you $2 worth of nickels and you'll end up spending that $2 plus more. However, you're no fool. You take the money and don't spend anything. Why it's even possible to go to Las Vegas, not gamble and come away with more money than you had when you left.

Other Cheap Vacation Fun

Fred considers nothing more enjoyable than lying on his couch and flipping the television channels. The couch is already paid for and so is the television set.

Fred is lucky because he genuinely doesn't want to go any place. When Fred was in his early twenties, he joined the Navy and saw the world. And after seeing the world that way, it pretty much took all the yearning to travel out of him.

Cheapskates who do travel, however, have one thing in common.

Motel Six.

They also find pleasure in the simple, inexpensive things.

Betty and Harry know all about Motel Six and every other discount motel on the way from Ohio to California where they drive to visit their daughter every year or two. They pack an ice chest in the back seat of their car and that way, they don't have to stop and buy anything but gas. Though Harry and Betty are not overly sociable people, they especially enjoy meeting people when they travel. The good thing about meeting people this way is that it doesn't last very long. And it doesn't involve exchanging birthday presents or bringing house warming gifts. You get the socializing but none of the expense.

Janette Wilson loves the shopping when she travels. Just shopping in a new supermarket excites her. She's taken all seven of her children on her trips. In fact, much of what the children know, they learned from motels. They learned how to operate an elevator in a motel and they learned how to swim in a motel swimming pool. They learned about ice buckets and ice machines, and what a maid is.

When Jim and Janette Wilson and their seven children drive up to a motel, the kids know what to do. Duck. It's simple. It means that they fling themselves against the floor until they'vedriven past the motel lobby. It's a precautionary measure taken in case someone inside the lobby is looking out and counting heads. Because while Janette Wilson is perfectly willing to pay for 2 motel rooms, she refuses to pay for 9 occupants. She pays the minimum and she asks for rooms towards the back. But if a path through the lobby is necessary, the children are trained on what to do. Wait for mother to go on her way and then follow her---not too close and one at a time. Forget Disney World, going to a motel is the greatest fun.

In the evening, they go to the nearest supermarket to buy supper. They have a picnic in the motel room, eating bologna sandwiches in bed, which they can't do at home. They race between the connecting doors of the two rooms and jump on the beds.

In the morning, it's time to pack and hit the road again for the next motel. Janette Wilson has her own method of packing and clearing out a motel room. She packs up every bar of soap (even the ones used last night in the shower) and all the toilet paper. Tough luck if you have to go to the bathroom after mom has packed. She takes the box of tissues, the stationery, the plastic cups, the plastic bags and every other disposable item left for guests. She also sends the children off to help themselves to soap and toilet paper off the maid's cart. To Janette Wilson's credit, she usually leaves the towels.

The Wilson's hold a lionized status amongst cheapskates. They are recognized for having crammed their whole family into a regular sized sedan and driven to Miami, Florida in August WITHOUT once turning on the air-conditioning. When they arrived back home, they had all lost a considerable amount of weight. But they had gained an enormous quantity of toilet paper, plastic cups, sanitary napkins bags (which lasted until Janette's oldest daughter was out of college), tissue boxes, soap and motel stationery.

Chapter Seventeen

Junk Car Bonds

Why is it when you see a person driving by in an expensive car, you think he's rich. While you see a person drive by in an old clunker and you think he's poor?

Now it may be true that the person driving the expensive car has more income than the person driving the junker, but a good piece of that income is going into a depreciating asset. But if what you're driving is a pile of junk, then that's when people should think, "Hey, here's a person who keeps all his money in the bank."

Junk cars just don't get much respect.

Rita and Fred have been driving junk cars for years and they always have to answer those same questions from disbelieving friends.

Aren't new cars more economical than junkers? Just how much do you spend on maintenance, friends ask.

As little as possible, they answer.

The goal is not to have a car that sounds perfect or that looks great. The main object is to have a car that runs. In fact, that's the only object. So, when Fred complains that the car doesn't sound right, Rita always says, "Don't listen to it". As she sees it, when you have a car older than your grown children, you shouldn't ask for much. Who complains about what a 105 year old woman sounds like? It's enough she's breathing.

It isn't safe to drive a junk car, their friends say.

It's true that they don't have air bags but then the rusted dashboards usually give way easily enough. And there's always the possibility of escape by falling through the floorboards.

And what about dependability? It seems that people believe that junk cars aren't as dependable as new cars.

Any mechanical device can fail, which brings up an old Abbott and Costello joke about homely girls. Lou Costello says he wants to marry a homely girl because a pretty girl is apt to run away. Can't a homely girl run away too, asks Bud. Sure, says Lou, but who cares? When a car you're still making monthly payments on quits in the middle of nowhere, it's just not the same as when a old junker that's paid for quits.

And what about pride and pleasure, friends always ask. There can't be the same pride and pleasure behind the wheel of a junker as behind the wheel of a nice shiny new car.

Well, let me tell you, Rita and Fred always say, that there is pride and pleasure in owning a junk car too. There is a pride in sitting in the seat, no matter how torn it is, because this is a car so out of date that no one bothers to steal it, so rusted that you don't have to buy any collision insurance, so old that you paid for it years and years ago. This is the kind of car that gives you true peace of mind.

And you just can't put a price tag on something like that!

Chapter Eighteen

Frugal Holiday Fun

For people that hate the holidays, you can always ignore them.

Or, you can live by relatives who don't mind the holidays and you can sponge off of them.

Or, you can celebrate the holidays yourself by doing the very minimum.

NEW YEAR'S EVE.

Go to sleep and forget about it.

VALENTINE'S DAY.

Remember love is spiritual, not material. Say I love you and be done with it.

JULY 4th.

Picnics aren't costly; fireworks are. You bring the hot dogs, let someone else bring the fireworks.

HALLOWEEN.

Halloween is a great holiday for cheapskates. It's the only one where you can get things free without first filling out any kind of financial statement.

Our old friend cheapskate Janette Wilson always has all her kids go out on Halloween. Costumes are easy. The girls pretend to be boys by wearing the boys' clothes; the boys pretend to be girls by wearing the girls' clothes. Then all seven of them hit the neighborhood to collect candy. And what does Janette Wilson do? She shuts off all the lights in her house and pretends not to be home. Then once her children come back with some goodies, she sorts through them, taking out the uncovered stuff and other candy no one eats. Then she'll turn on her lights and give these out to the neighborhood children.

As for Janette's children, they are a credit to her. If they ever find a house that gives out good stuff, like full-size candy bars, they keep visiting it until the owner refuses to treat them anymore.

THANKSGIVING.

Give thanks turkey is a cheap bird.

CHRISTMAS

Have you ever thought that your children have so many toys that you could probably re-wrap some of them and they wouldn't even realize on Christmas Day that they were getting something they already had?

Janette Wilson tried it one year.

The kids did know.

Every Christmas, Betty use to talk about giving money to the postman and the newspaper delivery person. Every Christmas, she talked about it. Sometimes she got as far as putting some money in an envelope. But she'd always take it out again. She figured that the postman was probably making more than she and Harry were.

When Betty has the grandchildren over to unwrap presents, they wouldn't dare tear the wrapping paper off. The wrapping paper is removed carefully---as if it were money, and the ribbons are stockpiled on a table. All of it will be used again next year.

In Janette Wilson's house, stockings on the fireplace say things like "to my dear aunt" and "to my darling niece". But don't think she has any aunts or nieces over for Christmas. Her own children get those stockings and they know which of them are the aunts and which are the nieces. And they also know why mom bought those wierd stockings. They were on sale, dirt cheap.

BIRTHDAYS

The very best present that Fred can get Rita---and he gets it for her every birthday, Valentine's Day and anniversary---is absolutely nothing. Rita's the type of wife who--if she found out that Fred had gone out with another woman---would be absolutely devastated that he had spent some money without checking with her first. Her first questions would be, where did you go? and how much did it cost you. At the bottom of her list of questions would be anything about what the other woman looked like....unless, of course, Fred had something to do with paying for that too.

CHILDREN'S BIRTHDAYS.

Start small---cake and ice cream with the family---and try to keep it that way. If you never make a monumental to-do over a child's birthday, he'll be none the wiser.

Chapter Nineteen

How to Be A Cheap But Gracious Hostess

When some people entertain, they bring out the best china, decorate the table with fresh flowers and fret about whether their guests will have enough to eat.

When Andrea entertains, she's apt to hide the bag of M & M's in the back of the cupboard and move the namebrand soda pop out of the refrigerator.

There is undoubtedly an art to being a gracious hostess.

But cheapskates only have to worry about two rules.

Rule one concerns the food.

There must be food. And it must be edible.

What kind of food you serve is determined by rule two: the guests you invite.

Most women will not turn down a free meal no matter what is being served. It only matters that they're are not the ones who are doing the serving. They could be ill and they'd still come, unless they couldn't find someone to carry them there.

Jean suffered a heart attack a month before her sister threw a dinner party. Jean had only been out of the hospital a couple of days but she managed to come to the party. She was weak. She couldn't help in putting away the dishes after the meal. But she was able to help herself to the food.

Betty use to enjoy going to dinner parties but she recently stopped going. She didn't mind getting the free food and beverage but she absolutely hated the reciprocating. She just decided it was cheaper for her to do without than to have to return the favor. However, she still does enjoy eating at her daughters' houses because, as she sees it, she already spent twenty years fulfilling her end of the rule of reciprocity. Now it's their turn.

Of course, some people don't feel any urge to reciprocate.

Rick is a divorced father of two and cheapskate extraordinaire. Rick never turns down a meal invitation. And it doesn't matter what you serve Rick, he'll eat it happily.

And that's the secret to rule number two as well as the secret on how to be a gracious hostess and still be cheap.

You've got to invite people even cheaper than you are and then you will have guests who marvel at your generosity.

Chapter Twenty

On the Blacktop Market, Things Are Dirt Cheap

How can you add volumes to your library for only a few dollars? Where can you indulge your children in any object they fancy with mere pocket change? From what can you bring home extravagant things you never thought you'd be able to afford (or want to)?

There's more than one answer.

Garage sales.

Flea markets.

Thrift shops.

It's usually in the springtime when the bargain hunters come out of hibernation and the bargain hunting of second-hand merchandise begins. The most well-known variety of garage sale is the tables-on-the-driveway affair with a homemade sign adorning the lawn. A far fancier variation on this theme is the professionally run tag sales in which the entire contents of a house are sold. The owners of these tag sale sites, which run from nice to magnificent homes with libraries and swimming pools, have sometimes died, or are getting a divorce or are just moving out of state. But who cares? The great prices are all that matters.

There is no general store as diversified as a good tag sale where a shopper can find antiques, clothing, televisions, dishes, bedroom sets, knickknacks as well as plants, rugs, lawn mowers, vacuum cleaners and jewelry. And few shopkeepers have ever displayed as much motivation as these tag/garage sale operators who want to move all the merchandise in a matter of hours. Towards the end of the sale, the question isn't what the operator wants to get but what the shopper wants to give.

Ilene is quite a vision at garage sales. She will fill her arms up with things she wants---books, dishes and straw baskets---and then she'll go up to the operator and say, "How about $2 for all this?"

Flea markets have lots of different operators competing with each other under one roof. Often there are stands featuring new merchandise alongside stands selling used merchandise and nearbystands selling fruits and vegetables. A shopper can buy a new T-shirt, handmade crafts, such as leather bags or wooden stools, used books as well as fresh lettuce, tomatoes, cucumbers and green peppers for a nice salad for lunch.

Whenever Cindy and Tom have friends or relatives visit them in Florida, they take them to the nearest flea market. That way, the friends and relatives can stock up on all sorts of souvenirs as gifts for the folks back home. And the folks don't have to know just how little was spent on them!

Thrift shops are popular hunting grounds too. Gloria takes her children there to shop, trying to instill in them, at an early age, a zest for bargains. It is possible to get very nice things at thrift shops because, while cheap people shop at thrift shops, it's generous people who supply the store's merchandise. Consequently, it is possible to buy something used at a thrift shop that is nicer than anything a cheap people would buy new. And if a good cause is being helped while also saving money, what's the harm?

Just as it's true that not everyone falls in love with the same person, it is also true that the same shopping experience will not satisfy each and every shopper.

But fortunately, this is a greatly diversified and enterprising country with everything from malls to warehouses to flea markets to outlets to depots to garage sales to street vendors.

Consequently, it is safe to conclude that there is probably a shopping experience out there just waiting to satisfy each and every shopper no matter how demanding or particular, and no matter how cheap.

Part Four

Cheap Deeds and Pulling Weeds

Chapter Twenty-one

Environmentally Cheap

Cheap people are finally having the last laugh. It's turned out that being cheap is good for the environment.

Now everyone is discovering that what their parents told them to do was right all along. It was cheap and it was right. You should not stand in front of the refrigerator with the door open. You also shouldn't leave the lights on after you've left a room and you shouldn't leave the water running. Cheap people all over the world have been vindicated.

Environmentalists recite the things you can do to save energy and water as though these ideas are original with them. Heck, cheap people have been doing all this stuff for years.

Betty and Harold always share the same bath water. Betty takes her bath first and then Harold takes his. That makes Harold never quite as clean as Betty, so they never reverse this procedure. Betty also has a water saving device on her washing machine. First, she'll do a wash of her sheets and maybe her underwear. And then, she'll use the same wash water to wash Harold's underwear.

The Wilson family have a coming-of-age ritual in which Jim Wilson instructs each child on the proper method of taking a shower. Jim learned how in the Navy. Turn the water on to get wet, then the water goes off while you soap up. Then turn the water on again for a quick rinse. Voila, you're done and at most you used a bucket of water.

The Wilson children are also trained at an early age not to flush the toilet. The game in their house is getting as many people as possible on one flush. And this rule is applicable day or night. Often, out of the darkness, a voice will be heard urging, "don't flush". An instruction the prospective flusher always obeys.

In addition to saving water, cheap people have always saved paper. Paper towels, for example, can be found lying about Jean's kitchen. They're on top of the microwave and the washer and dryer. Why are they lying all over the kitchen? They're drying out so they can be used again. A paper towel in Jean's household has a long and varied life span. It starts with Jean in the kitchen where it's used for wiping pots first, then the countertops and then the kitchen floor. Next it makes it's way to Herb in the garage where it's used on the lawnmower and car before finally--at last--it finds peace in pieces in the trash.

Janette Wilson teaches each child that toilet paper is due a certain respect. The tiniest amount can do the job adequately. And Janette never bothers with paper towels. She keeps the napkins used after a meal and saves those for wiping up spills and other messes.

Fred enriches the world by saving. Instead of throwing things down the garbage disposal, he throws it all into an empty milk container sitting by the kitchen sink. Fred uses eggshells, apple cores, banana peels, potato skins, and other organic products for a backyard compost heap. Best to keep it in the backyard just in case the neighbors aren't familiar with this type of farming. A compost heap will make use of "garbage" to produce soil rich in nutrients, which you can then distribute throughout your yard.

Keep the lights off unless you're using them, don't run the water or flush toilets until it is absolutely necessary, and use paper sparingly. Save money while you save the world.

Chapter Twenty-two

When Is It Time?

There is a time for every season, but the big question is when exactly is it time to turn on the air-conditioning.

For some people, this question is easy. They're uncomfortable; they feel a tad of heat generating on the nap of their neck. And that's all it takes for them to turn on the air-conditioning. For them, it is a simple flick of a switch with no need to pace back and forth to mull the decision. The fact that the air-conditioning is on is just the background against which their lives are played. Air-conditioning, for them, never takescenter stage.

But for a cheapskate, turning on the air-conditioning can be an endless source of discussion and discord, of scenes of anger and passion. A cheapskate could write a play in which the main conflict would be whether or not to turn on the air-conditioning. And then the next big question would be at what degree to set it.

At the least, it is certainly something to write home about.For mother and daughter, Ilene and Ellen, a big part of every letter concerns the status of the air-conditioner. "Haven't turned mine on yet," Ellen writes her mother, "since there is a pleasant breeze with the windows open."

"Had mine on the last two days, but open the windows at night," Ilene writes back. So it goes, until summer is over and then the big question becomes when to turn on the heat.

Fred believes that there is a valid scientific reason for not turning on the air-conditioner. Living in the heat, he says, helps you adjust better to living in the heat.

Living in the heat is, in fact, a point of pride with Fred. He frequently challenges people to a kind of duel as to just who can withstand the heat better. He suggests they mow lawns in the middle of the afternoon in August. The loser is the one who passes out first.

There is a method to a cheapskates' madness. They genuinely believe that there are less expensive ways to beat the heat. They may use electric fans. They may drink long, cool glasses of water. They may bathe repeatedly. They may lie quietly on the couch until the heat passes and they have regained consciousness.

Though cheapskates aren't generally nudists (where would they put their wallet?), for some, beating the heat involves a little nudity.

It is a fact that all over the country, there are people who walk around the house in little more than their underwear just to keep the air-conditioning off.

So if it takes a little time for some of them to answer their doors, you'll know why.

Chapter Twenty-three

Lawn Care, Who Cares?

Each homeowner is confronted with a host of important decisions to make. Not least among them is how many hours and how much money should he invest in dirt. To edge or not to edge, that is the question.

Dirt is big business. How to arrange the dirt, what to put in the dirt, keeping the dirt in place...all this occupies many hours that could be spent in a less expensive, more productive occupation. Like watching television.

One woman, Lucy, pays one set of men an extraordinary amount of money to cut her grass and then she pays another set of men an extraordinary amount of money to make her grass grow. This is the kind of expensive confusion displayed by many homeowners who become overly preoccupied with their yards.

It isn't only financially damaging for people to take too much pride in their lawn, it also isn't financially healthly for the neighbors.

One particularly frugal homeowner named Gary was trying to beat the high cost of sod and seed by letting his grass grow tall enough to seed itself. It seemed like a good idea, and it might have worked, only the neighbors objected before the grass was even a foot tall.

Most homeowners seem to regard grass as the sine qua non of suburban living even though low growing ivys and other low ground cover would be cheaper and easier. Consequently, they water; they fertilize; they bag; they rake; they edge; they prune; they mow; they seed and sod. The greener their lawns are, the less green you can be sure that their bank accounts are.

Still, if you have your heart set on grass, there is another issue that awaits you. Who cuts it? Since it costs money to hire someone to do it, obviously, it must be done by a loved one.

Some husbands take on this task themselves. They believe that mowing and other lawn care is men's work. (God bless them.)

Other men think that lawn work can be done by either sex since mowers don't particularly care who operates them. Fred says he's willing to cut the lawn....whenever the grass gets tall enough.

If you want to keep your lawn care costs down, you've got to either do it yourself or, preferably, have your spouse do it. If both of you absolutely hate doing it, you have only one option open to you. You have got to lower your standards.

What you've got to cultivate most is a different attitude. You should try to view your yard through the eyes of a naturalist. A naturalist observes nature; he doesn't try to change it.

Plants in the natural world do not come in neat round shapes. You must purchase shears to get them in those shapes. It also isn't natural to find precise distinctions between the area of grass and the area of shrubbery. This requires edging equipment.

Your precisely symmetrical and geometric yard is not only expensive, it is not natural. And if it's not natural, it's unecological. And in being unecological, it means you're wasting energy. And if you are wasting energy, you are wasting money.

Your yard should reflect the natural world experiences. If it's alive, then, obviously, conditions in your yard are conducive to its living. And if it doesn't thrive in the sun and rain it gets, then it doesn't deserve to live.

As for edging, the only edges you should be concerned about come in sets of four, are green and have the presidents' portraits inside them.

Chapter Twenty-four
CMO (Chief Maintenance Officer)

Every home no matter how humble has a member designated as Chief Maintenance Officer. In really thrifty households, this rank might be more accurately referred to as Cheap Maintenance Officer.

The duties of a CMO are essential to a home's operation and, though a CMO does not earn money from the jobs he performs, he does something even more important--- he saves money. The CMO keeps household operations at peak, cheap performance by, first, maintaining in stock every imaginable item. If a request is made for an item as in, "My shoeslaces just broke", the competent CMO will produce the necessary item.

It is, of course, the CMO's job to ANTICIPATE what requests may arise. Although there may be a futility to this, the CMO must still try.

For example, in Betty and Harry's household, Harry seems to have a kind of sixth sense as to exactly what Betty has failed to purchase. "Got any chocolate chip cookies with raisins," he'll ask.

"I have chocolate chip cookies. I have cookies with raisins. I have raisins without cookies, chocolate without raisins, raisins with chocolate."

"But no chocolate chip cookies with raisins?" Harry repeats.

There is, of course, an art to shopping, much related to the art of anticipation. You must buy it when you don't need it. To be precise, you must buy it when you don't need it and don't want it and you can't even imagine needing it or wanting it. But you must buy it if it is something that you know you will need eventually. You've got to THINK SALES.

It's because most people buy things when they need them, that you can get such good prices when you don't need them. It's when the stores know everyone is thinking "swimsuits" that you get good prices on snowsuits and boots. They know they've got to coax you to buy for next season. Let's hope they continue to think people think that way because cheap people know the only time to shop is at the end of season clearance sale. And, an even better time to shop is at the end of the end of season clearance sales. Then, the stores are practically paying you to take the stuff away.

Of course, CMO's don't just stock up on clothes. They have their eye out for sales of all kinds. If they own a car, they look for sales on essentials like motor oil, transmission fluid, windshield wiper fluid and antifreeze. If they live any place other than a hotel or motel, they need to stock up on lightbulbs, vaccuum bags, laundry detergent, dishwasher detergent, shaving cream, toothpaste, soap, shampoo and so forth.

Ilene is a CMO Extraordinaire. If awards were given out for stocking up and buying cheap, Ilene would get a Lifetime Achievement Award because that's how much she has in stock...a lifetime's worth. Open her bathroom cabinets and rolls of toilet paper pour out. She has a downstairs closet filled with dishwasher detergents and laundry detergents of every kind. Boxes and bottles. The one thing they all have in common is a incredibly good price. Ilene also has an upstairs closet filled with hand lotion, toothpaste, shampoo and soap. When her children come to visit her or she visits them, she's apt to bring along gifts like a year's worth of hand cream or a bag of socks. If the price is right, Ilene buys in bulk. All CMO's salute you, Ilene.

The key word to a CMO's duties is not just shopping. It is also KEEPING.

Let's say a screw falls out of a vaccum and gets sucked up. Does a good CMO like Ilene find a replacement screw from among her stock of brand new screws? No. She would first check her collection of used screws. As CMO, you must not only save money, you must save everything. Ilene saves used shoelaces, buttons, empty detergent bottles, glass spaghetti bottles and many many other things. You don't have to buy containers for your leftovers. You just use the containers you bought food in. Frozen whip cream containers and cottage cheese containers can all serve this purpose.

In addition to stocking items, the other aspect of being a CMO involves repairing items. The area of repair is complicated by the fact that it requires a judgement call. Of course, shopping requires a lot of judgement calls too. (Will your daughter fit into the bargain priced snowsuit a year from now?) However, repairing usually involves more money.

When it comes to repairing, you must decide first whether it is more economical to repair it or to just live with another broken down piece of junk. For example, if a bicycle tire is broken, you'll probably have to repair it in order to use the bike. But if it's the bell on the bike that's broken, heck, you've probably got a set of good healthy lungs that will work just as well.

If you've decided that the thing should be repaired, the next question is "can you do the work yourself?" Or, better yet, can you get your spouse to do it?

Jan occasionally succeeds in getting her husband to do it although lately she's begun doing it herself instead. Her husband, Bill, believes in the Mutual Suffering Theory of Home Maintenance. If he is suffering fixing something, he wants his wife beside him suffering too. And just to make sure his wife's suffering is genuine, he will occasionally interrupt his work toreward her with an observation on married life and the pleasures thereof.

If you attempt to repair things yourself, you are bound to encounter the cheap man's eternal dilemma. You always need tools to do the job yourself; tools cost money; money is what you're trying to save by doing the job yourself. Thus it is that a cheap man is never really able to repair anything....although that has never stopped anyone truly cheap yet from trying.

What cheap people must do instead involves jerry-rigging things. This means taping, bending, gluing, and otherwise finangling things to work without replacing anything.

It is possible to hire someone else to repair whatever it is, though this is a last resort after all possible jerry-rigging (including kicking) has failed. Be sure to call around before settling on any one repairman. Though you may not know whether you've hired the greatest repairman on earth, at least make sure you've hired the cheapest. Remember, as CMO, it's your duty.

Chapter Twenty-five

Sometimes Depend on the Kindness of Strangers

It is undeniably true that there are generous people in this world. There are people who want to give you things but they're afraid you might be insulted. You have to soothe these sensitive souls. You have to reassure them that you are strong enough to take everything they have to give you and not feel the least bit humiliated.

Neighbors, for example, have clothes that their children have outgrown. You might ask them what they do with these clothes. If they don't have any idea, you might give them a few. You can even offer to pay them something for the clothes, though you want to be certain beforehand that they're much too generous to accept it.

Garage sales and flea markets are big draws for bargain seekers who depend on the kindness and sometimes the stupidity of strangers. But not all cheap people enjoy getting bargains this way. Cheap people come in varieties just like everyone else and some of them aren't interested in any bargain that has to be hunted for. They prefer the bargains that can be purchased over the phone and delivered direct to their door.

Those who don't enjoy the hunt have to rely on the kindness of relatives and neighbors. But for those people who do, there are lots of truly generous people out there and they take great pleasure in giving and helping others.

Find them and make them your friends.

Chapter Twenty-six

Cheap Morals, Tactics, and Strategy

It is probably easier for a rich person to be moral than it is for a poor person. A rich person doesn't need the money that a cashier might have overpaid him. A rich person doesn't have to steal to get what he wants. Money means only something to a rich person; but it means everything to a poor person.

By the same reasoning, it is also true that it is far easier for an extravagant person to be moral than it is for a cheapskate.

The main player in the battle of ethics each cheapskate wages is---let's face it---the sales clerk.

Sales clerks make mistakes. It doesn't matter how fancy that machine they punch numbers into is. They will still make mistakes. Thank god.

Sometimes sales clerks give the wrong change. Or, they figure out the math wrong. Janette remembers when she bought some clothes at 20% off. The salesperson rang up the first item and then took 20% off. She rang up the second item, totaled the two items and took 20% off.

Janette knew immediately what was going on. The sales person was taking 20% of what she had already taken off 20%.

On another occasion, Janette was buying dresses for her daughters. She bought two of the larger size and one at the small size. The small size was less expensive than the large size. The salesclerk mistakenly charged her two at the small size and only one at the large size.

Should Janette have said something in these situations? Should she have brought these errors to the salesclerk's attention?

Shouldn't the store be punished for hiring incompetent sales people?

Janette likes to think of it this way. She likes to say that she subscribes to the Conscience Theory of Salespersons. This means that the salesperson serves as her conscience. And, therefore, if it's okay with the salesperson, it's okay with her.

In those situations, Janette wasn't going out of her way to do something illegal. On the other hand, whenever Jean and Herb go out to eat, they always buy only one cup of coffee. And it's not because only one of them is a coffee drinker. It's because they go to eat at places with unlimited refills. That way, they pay for only one cup and they both drink out of it. They also do things like order an all-you-can-eat salad bar and share it.

Sometimes doing what isn't perfectly legal is hard to resist. For example, Janette Wilson always buys toilet paper when it goes on sale and it is always limited to something like 3 rolls per customer. Three rolls of toilet paper doesn't go very far in a family of nine. So, Janette Wilson has her own procedure for buying the toilet paper. She goes in and buys her three rolls. Then she sends the next child in to buy 3. Then another child goes in to buy

3 and so on. As Janette sees it, although the store may disagree, there isn't just one customer in her family.

There are all sorts of other cheap ways for getting what you want.

Fred wanted a subscription to a certain expensive magazine. So when the magazine offered 3 free issues with no obligation to buy anymore, he sent away for it. Naturally, the magazine kept coming even after the 3 issues had arrived. And Fred eventually got a dunning notice even though he had written cancel on the order just like he was supposed to do. He never did pay and, technically, what he did was legal. However, the magazine does intend its offer to be accepted only by those persons seriously considering getting a subscription. And Fred wasn't.

Oh, the things we do for money.

Mary, for example, never wanted to get married. It was just a promise she made to herself when she was a young girl. She had vowed to live her life without succumbing to that archaic ritual. So even though she loved Tom, she told him "no" when he asked her to marry him. And every time, Tom came up with a new argument, she persisted in saying "no". He told her how much his parents wanted to see him married because he was their last child who was still single. It was an embarrassment for them to tell the relatives that their over thirty son wasn't married. But Mary refused to budge. Then Tom told her how much being married would mean to him. But Mary said she was sorry but she couldn't relinquish her principles even for him. Then, one day, Tom happened to mention that the G. I. Bill would pay them $50 more each month if they were married. Now that, Mary said, was a damn powerful argument. And they were married the very next day.

Money vs. morals.

Price vs. principles.

Alas, it would be so easy for someone who wasn't cheap.

Chapter Twenty-seven

A Summing Up: The Big Question

Why?

Why out of all possibility choices should a person choose to be cheap?

What real difference does it make?

First, it's true that money can't buy happiness. And that means that neither can you.

If you're miserable deep down in your soul, a new car won't change it. And a big house alone isn't going to put a smile on your face. It might help in making you less miserable but it is not the whole answer.

And as for what real difference does being cheap make, why don't we compare bank statements.

But doesn't that seem contradictory?

You're being cheap in order to make money and then you go and say something totally confusing about money not buying happiness. How does this make any sense?

Let's put things in perspective.

First, you're cheap as a method and means to finding happiness. It takes being cheap to learn what makes you happy. You learn first to find happiness without spending any money. And you do that by getting down to the basics. You find it from within yourself. You find it from enjoying your spouse and your children, your family and your friends. You get it from the sound of rain on the roof and the sound of your car starting.

These are the simple, inexpensive things that should give you pleasure.

Concentrate on mastering them. Revel in them.

And then once you've learned that you can be happy with very little, you'll have discovered the true happiness that money can't buy.

And having done that, you're ready to learn that while money can't in itself buy happiness, it can bring you more of what you've already got.

Be cheap, gain wisdom and happiness. And if in the process, you accumulate vast wealth, all the better.

Part Five

A Cheapstake's Dictionary and Guide Book

ANAL-RETENTIVE: Freud's rationalization for his overspending.

APPEARANCES: Unimportant. Appearances do not determine wealth; bank accounts do.

AUTOMOBILE: a means to an end. You are not what you drive.

BARGAIN: What every cheap person is looking for.

CHARITY: Not only starts at home, but ends at home.

CHEAPNESS: Not a momentary impulse; it's a way of life.

CLOTHES: Children's clothes should only fit well one year out of three. The first year they should be too big; the middle year, they fit fine; the last year, they're getting small.

COUPONS: important but not as important as price.

CURTAINS: Sheets. Anyone who has checked the price of curtains lately knows that they are overpriced. Sheets are great-looking and can be converted into a curtain with little effort.

DIETING: Not eating. Translated this means eating LESS. It does not mean eating special foods that cost more money; it does not mean paying someone to talk to for support. It's supposed to decrease your waistline and increase your credit line.

DOG: A living replacement for a garbage disposal. All those horrible leftovers you usually feed your husband, can now be fed to this animal, which is how it became known as man's best friend.

ECOLOGIST: Something to call yourself if you're tired of cheapskate. Also conservationist.

EXERCISE: Stand up, bend down. If you want something more vigorous, go outside and start walking. If you want something even more vigorous, start running. You do not need fancy shoes or fancy clothes. You do not need a club or organization. If you can't find the discipline to exercise without spending any money, then there's no point spending any money.

EXPENSIVE: Bad.

FLOWERS: 1-800-DONT-BUY. Grow them yourself.

FREE: Good. (see expensive).

FUN: must be inexpensive. If it's expensive, it can't be fun.

GIFT: When a cheapskate gives one, it's the thought that counts most.

HAIRCUTS: Urban or rural. The rural haircut is given by a loved one, including yourself. To get an urban haircut, check the yellow pages of your telephone book for Barber Schools or Beauty Schools. These places usually offer all their services for amazingly low prices. Your local community college may also have a Cosmetology School, which does the same thing. Students do the cutting (or whatever) while instructors supervise. Though there is no guarantee in quality, in all the years I've been going, I've only had my hair butchered once. But it only cost $2 and the bald spot grew out very nicely.

IGNORANCE: Lack of knowledge, particularly of sales or other good deals, which may result in missing out on some great buys.

INSURANCE: is insurance that you'll have someone to sue when the company won't pay up. The main object in getting insurance is not to make the insurance company rich. High deductibles, minimum coverage and prayers to God all help.

INVESTMENTS: Sure, fine. Do it. Just don't lose any money.

JUNK MAIL: No such thing. Janette Wilson saves all envelopes and paper with at least one blank side to use as scratch paper for writing messages by the telephone or shopping lists.

KARATS: Never mind.

KETCHUP: all bottles, also roll-on deoderants, should be turned upside down and they will last to the very last drop.

KIN: Free meal.

LOVE: see money.

MALL: mauled.

MARRIAGE: a union created to pay less taxes.

MATERNITY CLOTHES: your husband's.

MONEY: see love.

NECESSARY: what most things aren't.

OUTLET STORE: a place to let out your shopping urges.

PLASTIC SURGERY: Don't worry about how big your nose is; don't worry about how big your thighs are; don't worry about how big your breasts are. How big is your investment portfolio?

PRICE:
QUALITY: Know these P's and Q's. You want quality and quantity
QUANTITY: at a low price.

RELATIVES: see kin.

RICH: what we are all trying to become.

SALE: fun.

TELEPHONE: it's not cellular, mobile or portable. It's in the house, one line, no call waiting. And no long distance phone calls are made without a stopwatch.

USED: the way to buy cars and furniture.

VACATION: an exploration of familiar places in and around the house.

WAITING: a virtue.

WINDOW TREATMENT: what color sheet?

X: a chromosome that has been traced to being cheap.

ZERO: your daily spending goal.

About the Author

Ann M. Rogers is a daughter, sister, wife, mother, homemaker, writer and bankruptcy attorney. During her life, she has experienced, and dealt with, fathers, mothers, brothers, sisters, husbands, wives, daughters, sons, uncles, aunts, nephews, nieces, friends, co-workers, clients and other sundry human beings from solvent billionaires to the bankrupt to bankrupt billionaires. She has experienced, and dealt with, their many personalities, loves, hates, cheapnesses, extravagances, hopes, joys, addictions, sufferings and their many and varied financial habits. She has lived in Michigan, New York, Maryland, California, Ohio and she currently lives in Florida.

Her formative years were spent studying philosophy and the law, both as an undergraduate, graduate and law school student. From her vast and varied experiences, vast and varied education and keen, insightful intelligence, she has created and formulated an economical, and fiscally sound, philosophy of life—cheapness. She has discovered that, from suffering billionaires to the joyfully bankrupt, there is one common factor to their happiness or suffering—cheapness. She has determined that to be truly happy or sad, and for fiscal immortality, one must embrace cheapness regardless of one's financial status. She has spent a lifetime exploring, in its many and varied aspects, cheapness as the only true modern philosophical lifestyle. She has now written the results of her unending quest for the perfect life with the perfect philosophy in her seminal work—Talk's Cheap...And So Am I. It is the definitive, authoritative, official guide to cheapness.